PEACE through PLANNING

— & —

the **8** truths you need to know about estate planning

CHARLES WEISINGER

ALEXANDRIA
VIRGINIA

Peace Through Planning
by Charles Weisinger

Published by:
Powerhouse Publishing
950 N. Washington Street
Alexandria, Virginia 22314

info@powerhousepublishing.net
703-595-4135

Copyright © 2019 by Charles Weisinger

All rights reserved. No part of this book may be reproduced or transmitted in any form or by any means, electronic or mechanical, including photocopying, recording, or by any information storage and retrieval system, except in the case of brief quotations embodied in critical articles and reviews, without prior written permission of the publisher. For more information contact: www.weisingerlawfirm.com

The author has made every effort to ensure the accuracy of the information within this book was correct at time of publication. The author does not assume and hereby disclaims any liability to any party for any loss, damage, or disruption caused by errors or omissions, whether such errors or omissions result from accident, negligence, or any other cause. The information contained within this book is strictly for educational purposes. If you wish to apply ideas contained in this book, you are taking full responsibility for your actions. The information is strictly given as the author's statements and is not meant to be taken as financial advice. Please consult a financial professional before making a change.

Printed in the United States of America

ISBN Paperback Edition: 9781694966230

Cover Design: Bruce Coderre
Interior Design: Bruce Coderre

To my beautiful wife Olivia and to our amazing children Jack, Lincoln, Charlie, Gabriel, and to our baby boys Hudson and Parker who completed their races early. I am looking forward to our reunion my precious buddies.

CONTENTS

	Introduction: Why we plan	1
TRUTH #1	A good estate plan is one that you understand...................	5
TRUTH #2	Like and trust your attorney or choose someone else	9
TRUTH #3	You should name people you trust............	17
TRUTH #4	No one will care for your kids the way you do, but you can still make the best available choice	25
TRUTH #5	Adults need wills	29
TRUTH #6	Probate stinks..............................	33
TRUTH #7	Trusts are neither scary nor expensive........	41
TRUTH #8	Your lawyer should know your team	47
BONUS TRUTH #1	Special needs require special planning	51
BONUS TRUTH #2	The estate tax will not directly affect most Americans	55

ESTATE PLANNING QUESTIONNAIRE
Helping you achieve peace
through planning........................... 59

INTRODUCTION:
WHY WE PLAN

As a father of four young boys, I think about their safety and security every single day. I wake up in the morning with my boys at the front of my mind. Where are they going today? Do we have enough milk? Is it my day to drop them at school or is it my wife's day? Our four boys have only three years in between them. This means our home is often a crazy and loud place. For example, one recent morning, our twins got up before my wife and me. By the time we emerged from our room, our twins had taken a fork and opened several bags of chips. The sound of the pop and the spray of chips provided enormous amounts of glee. The only room in the house untouched by broken chips was our bedroom. Later that same day, three of our four boys decided they wanted to see who could scream the loudest while my wife was sitting with them in the car waiting for me to come out of the house.

Even though I am constantly thinking about my children, our hectic lives leave us with little time to think about, much less plan for, their future needs. However, when we do think about their future, we envision our boys growing up and going to college, finding a special someone, and getting married and having children of their own. As a dad, I look forward to watching every step of the way and guiding my boys in the best way I can.

Life doesn't always go as we plan. Sometimes, life throws us a curveball. That curveball might be an unexpected illness, accident, or even death. While these are things we don't like to talk about, they are a natural part of life and must be discussed and planned for.

I am reminded of the children's movie, The Lion King and its theme song, "The Circle of Life". Mufasa planned to spend a lot of time teaching his son the ways of the lion and how to be a great leader but fell short in the planning department. When Mufasa died unexpectedly, little Simba was left to learn the ways of the world on his own. He was first influenced by his evil uncle, Scar, and then eventually fell in with some rowdy friends who meant well, but didn't lead Simba to the place he was supposed to be. Had Mufasa taken more time to plan, he could have put others in place to immediately step in and care for Simba in the way he would have. Mufasa could have made it clear to the rest of the pack that Scar was not to be left in charge. He could have created a succession plan laying out who would guard the throne until Simba was able to assume the throne himself.

This story is not unique to children's movies, although it is a theme that is repeated many times throughout cinema. Just take a few moments to flip through the movies on the Hallmark channel every holiday season. Many films feature a struggling widow trying to make the ends meet and care for her child or children. Good planning doesn't make great television or movies. You are not likely to see a movie about the family who lost their patriarch, visited the attorney and life insurance agent, and realized they had a plan in place ensuring that college was going to be affordable. A movie about a family allowed to focus on grieving and caring for each other rather than fighting with each other is not likely to sell many tickets. However, I don't care if my family ever makes the news or has our life story turned into a made for prime time television special. I want my family to be able to continue living and caring for one another whether or not I am here. I want to provide them with lasting safety and security. I bet you do too. That is what Estate Planning is about. Sure, there are strategies to make sure that the government doesn't get any more tax dollars and we can talk about advanced life insurance trusts and other vehicles. However, at the end of the day, what matters is that your family is able to be cared for as you wish. The goal of this book is to help you and your family achieve "Peace Through Planning".

> **I don't care if my family ever makes the news or has our life story turned into a made for prime time television special. I want my family to be able to continue living and caring for one another whether or not I am here.**

TRUTH 1

A GOOD ESTATE PLAN
IS ONE THAT YOU
UNDERSTAND

First and foremost, a good estate plan is a plan that you understand. As an estate planning attorney, I often meet with clients who bring me a plan they created years ago. Often, the plan was prepared by an attorney with whom they had no relationship and have not spoken to since they received the documents. I ask them how their plan is set up and what it is supposed to accomplish. Unfortunately, many of these clients do not remember what the plan is or how it works.

I spoke with a client recently who brought in a stack of papers and laid them on the table in front of me. She said, "This is the trust that my daughter's attorney set up for me." Her statement set off several alarms in my head, but at this juncture, we are going to focus on just one of those flags. She said, "The trust set up for me." I wondered if she had made any decisions about what was in the trust. I started with, "What is the purpose of your trust? What is it intended to accomplish?" Unfortunately, she had no idea. Her eyes filled with tears as the emotion bubbled over. Her daughter told her that she needed it, scheduled the appointment, and took her mom to the lawyer's office to sign it. Mom now knew she had a plan, but she had no idea what was in it. It wasn't her plan. The plan may have been perfect; it may have accomplished exactly what Mom wanted. However, the plan brought her no peace because she didn't understand it. When she read the documents, she became confused by all the legalese. Her wishes were not honored in the document simply because no one bothered to ask what her wishes were.

Simply reading the documents does not always help. In fact, many documents are simply too confusing. I have reviewed trust documents that contain hundreds of pages, which take me hours to go through and understand, and I practice estate planning every day! If it is difficult for an attorney to understand, how are the executors and beneficiaries supposed to carry it out? An effective estate plan should be one that can be carried out and understood by those who are tasked with executing it. That is not to say that there shouldn't be some complex provisions to maximize the benefits, whether those benefits revolve around tax protections or complex distribution provisions. However, it is imperative that you know what is in your plan.

It is imperative that you know what is in your plan.

TRUTH 2

LIKE AND TRUST
YOUR ATTORNEY OR
CHOOSE SOMEONE
ELSE

At the risk of sounding corny and simple, I am going to say it plainly: the most important decision in choosing an estate planning attorney is choosing someone you enjoy and feel comfortable talking to. If you have reservations about sharing information with your attorney, you may withhold important pieces of the puzzle from him or her. That can lead to disaster in the future. For example, if you are not comfortable sharing your financial data, including your salary, the money in your retirement accounts, etc., your attorney will not be able to complete the picture and make sure your estate is covered. If the attorney walks in the room and your first thought is, "This guy is after my money", then stand up, politely excuse yourself and run for the door. Find someone new. While most estate plans can be set up in as little as two face-to-face meetings, you want to feel comfortable calling and asking questions or coming back to make updates over time. I recently had a client tell me she was very nervous about meeting with me but was so relieved when I walked in the room because I wasn't fat. She said she had never trusted fat doctors and fat lawyers. I thanked her for not thinking I was fat, went back to my office, and started shopping

> **The most important decision in choosing an estate planning attorney is choosing someone you enjoy and feel comfortable talking to.**

for a treadmill. While she may not have thought I was fat, I have definitely been on an upward trajectory since my college days. While that is a somewhat silly example, it confirms the point that you have to feel comfortable with your attorney or you won't share your most important information with him or her.

My grandmother once went to a doctor my dad recommended. My grandmother was eighty-two years old at the time. In his first meeting with my grandmother, the doctor commented as he examined her, "My, that is a big belly!" My dad had to force her to go back the next time she became ill. I was only ten years old at the time, but I remember hearing the story and finding it unbelievable that a doctor would be so rude and careless to a patient.

In a similar vein, clients have told me stories of lawyers who have drafted plans and never stopped to ask the client what their goals were. Another client of mine fired her CPA after he gave her advice she questioned. He retorted, "Well, you have the money. Why are you worried about it?" She quickly let him know that she only had the money she did, because she paid attention and "worried" about it. Your Estate Planning Attorney should spend most of the initial meeting learning about the goals you have for your family and property. They should then educate you and help ensure that you leave there with much better clarity and direction for your specific plan.

Remember, you are paying for their services, which means you are in the driver's seat. You determine what goes into your plan, and you should choose an advisor who realizes and remembers that. I recently had a client who came to me with a request which I thought was probably not the best idea. I counseled him as to what the different options were. Ultimately, he decided he wanted to continue with a course of action I recommended against. In this example, I advised my client to file an estate tax return in order to potentially save money in the future through a portability election. In short, my advice would have potentially saved hundreds of thousands of dollars in the future at his death by filing this return. He decided that he didn't want to mess with it since the cost would be paid after his death and not by him. It was my job to advise him of the options, but ultimately it was his choice to make. Sometimes, advisors forget that they don not get to make the decisions; they can only recommend them. When choosing an Estate Planning Attorney, choose one who spends more time listening than talking. However, also choose one that will challenge you to think in different ways.

Last, but certainly not least important, is understanding that Estate Planning is a specialty area of the law that involves putting a plan in place to take care of what is most important to you. It is not an area that should be taken lightly. It should not be an attorney's side practice or something they do some of the time. It should be their area of focus. As an Estate Planning Attorney, I would never recommend you hire me if you were charged with a crime or were hurt by a big trucking company. Hiring me in those legal areas would likely result in you spending time in jail or losing out on a great deal of money. It often troubles me to hear that a criminal defense or personal injury attorney just threw a Will together for a client. We may all have the same license hanging on the wall, but that doesn't mean we all have adequate knowledge to help in every area.

Most of law school is spent teaching students how to think like lawyers and how to pass the Bar Examination. In fact, there are few classes in law school directed towards Estate Planning and Probate law. I took one class in law school titled, "Wills and Estates". Would you believe that when I graduated from law school, I had never drafted a single Will or Trust as part of my education? I gained some exposure to the area only by taking a part-time job with a local attorney who practiced Estate Planning. So, if attorneys don't learn this in law school, where do they learn it? They learn in two places. The first is by reading books and practicing what they learn on clients. The second is by immersing themselves in the community of Estate Planning Attorneys, joining forces with other attorneys and undertaking frequent and consistent continuing education classes. In Texas, the State Bar of Texas hosts several courses every year that range from basic estate planning principles to advanced strategies and techniques. Additionally, there are national courses where the brightest in the field come together to discuss the latest and best practices.

Here are a few ways to make sure that you are choosing an Estate Planning Attorney who will serve you well. First, look at their website. Do they have any additional certifications listed? How long have they been practicing?

If they are fairly new, do they work closely with a seasoned attorney? Are they a member of any organizations that focus on Estate Planning? Any attorney can join The National Association of Estate Planners and Councils, which is a fantastic start, as the council provide countless resources and a network of professionals to lean. However, that attorney can also go further and achieve the Accredited Estate Planner designation which takes some additional experience and study to obtain. Is this their area of focus or just one of the areas they practice in? Second, Google their name. Do they have any client reviews? Client reviews will often tell you a lot about how the attorney interacts with their clients and whether people leave merely satisfied or become Raving Fans![1] Third, ask your Certified Financial Planner (CFP) for a recommendation. Your financial advisor will likely have a few attorneys with whom they have worked that have taken good care of their other clients. They will likely also have a few that they can tell you to steer clear of.

Are they Board Certified in Estate Planning and Probate law? In order to be Board Certified by the Texas Board of Legal Specialization, an attorney has to have been licensed for a minimum of 5 years, spent at least 25% of their time practicing in the specialty area, obtained judicial recommendations, peer recommendations, and passed a very difficult test in the specialty area. **Less than 10% percent of all attorneys in Texas are Board Certified in any given area**

---

[1] Blanchard, Ken. 1993. Raving Fans: A Revolutionary Approach to Customer Service. New York, NY. William Morrow and Company, Inc.

and less than 1% of all Texas attorneys are Board Certified in Estate Planning and Probate.[2]

Therefore, you can rest assured that by choosing a Board Certified attorney you are at a minimum choosing an attorney who is competent in this area of practice.

---

[2] Texas Board of Legal Specialization. (n.d). Retrieved from www.tbls.org/Defaul.aspx

TRUTH

YOU SHOULD NAME
PEOPLE YOU TRUST

Now that you have picked your attorney, you get to start making more decisions, such as who to name in all of your documents. Choosing who to name for the potential jobs in your estate plan is where a lot of people get stumped. In the Seinfeld episode, *The Comeback: Coma*, Kramer struggles with the decision of who should be his Medical Power of Attorney. He has made the decision that he doesn't want to be left on life support, and he wants his agent to remove the "life support, feeding tube, lung blower, etc.". He first considers his friend, Jerry, but decides Jerry has too much difficulty letting go. Kramer then turns to another friend, Elaine. He believes Elaine is a good fit as she is a "calculating cold-hearted businesswoman who doesn't mind stomping on a few throats." As good comedies often do, they take a serious conversation and help us look at it with some humor.

Our clients often ask how to choose the right person to be their executor, medical power of attorney, etc. Here are a few pointers on choosing the right person for each job.

The Executor should be someone whom you know to be fair-minded and able to set aside personal biases.

The Executor and Trustee. The Executor named in your Will has the responsibility of making sure that your assets get to the beneficiaries you choose. In the case of a Trust, the Trustee takes the job of managing the assets for the benefit of the beneficiary. The most important thing to remember when choosing an Executor or Trustee is that the person's job is to get the assets to the beneficiaries. This person's job has nothing to do with taking care of you or making sure that someone else's feelings don't get hurt. The first step is determining who your beneficiaries are. The second step is choosing who will do the best job getting the assets to them.

The Executor should be someone whom you know to be fair-minded and able to set aside personal biases. This person will be tasked with carrying out exactly what is in the written document, regardless of what they might personally feel should happen. The Executor will often be approached by family members or friends who will say things like, "My mother always wanted me to have her spotted dolphin earrings!" or "Dad told me he wanted me to receive twenty thousand dollars to start my new business. He was going to give me a check next week." The Executor needs to be a person who can stand firm and abide by the written documents, regardless of their personal emotions. If it is not in the document, it doesn't happen.

It should go without saying that this person should be proficient with finances. If you have an uncle who has claimed bankruptcy a few times, he is probably not the best choice to handle your estate, no matter how nice he is. If you are going to choose a family member or friend, choose someone who actually knows how much money they have in the bank at a given time. If your friend calls the bank every morning to determine if he can afford to put gas in the car, the job of Executor would likely be overwhelming.

One of my favorite sayings is, "If you want something done quickly, find a busy person and ask them to do it." If your best friend is a well-known procrastinator, do not saddle them with this job. If you have that friend who loves to organize and create file folders and labels for all of them, that person may be a better choice as Executor. The job of Executor or Trustee takes someone who can methodically go through items and bank accounts and sort everything out. The beneficiaries will be calling to find out when they will receive their distributions sooner than you might think. We live in a society where many, if not most, people live paycheck to paycheck. The promise of money coming from any source starts as excitement but quickly turns to frustration if they do not receive their money quickly after it is promised. The Executor or Trustee needs to show that they are methodically going through the process to get the funds to the beneficiary and simultaneously be able to calm them long enough to get the job completed.

That being said, the person you choose does not have to be a genius. They don't have to have formal training in law, accounting, or money management. They should, however, be someone who will look to professionals in those areas for guidance and follow their advice.

"Depending on the complexity of your estate, you may wish to appoint a professional, such as a CPA, Attorney, or Financial Institution." Linda Namestnik was a long-time trust officer at Frost Bank. She recently retired. In my first-ever meeting with her, she mentioned that naming a Corporate Trustee often brings the family closer together, because when the family gets together for Thanksgiving Dinner, they can all agree that they hate the Trustee. The first time I heard her say that, I was a fairly new attorney and I thought it was a strange comment. Through my experience, I now understand fully what she meant. Regardless of who the Trustee is, there are likely going to be people who don't feel like they are doing the best job. If that Trustee is also a family member, it can breed discord among other family members. As Dave Ramsey likes to say, when there are money issues between family members, "the turkey just tastes different."

Financial Power of Attorney. A lot of what was stated in regard to the Executor could be repeated when determining whom to name as your Financial Power of Attorney. This person has the job of handling your money for you in the case that you become unable to do so for any reason. Again, this person should be someone you trust completely and is very good at record keeping. Early in my career, I served as an attorney ad litem representing an elderly woman whose daughters were fighting over who should be her caretaker. My client, the mother, was completely incapacitated due to Alzheimer's dementia. One daughter lived locally and had been caring for her mother for the preceding ten years, even before her mother lost capacity. She bought groceries and always drove her mother to all her appointments. As I investigated, I found and believed there was no evidence of any wrongdoing on her part. However, she also had not kept any records for those ten years. Her sister believed she was stealing from their mother and brought a lawsuit to have the local sister removed as Power of Attorney and Trustee. While there was likely no wrongdoing, it was a difficult case for the court because one of the duties of an agent serving under a power of attorney is to account for their actions. Had the local daughter kept records of all the spending, there would have been no question, and the court would have quickly thrown the case out.

> Depending on the complexity of your estate, you may wish to appoint a professional, such as a CPA, Attorney, or Financial Institution.

<u>Medical Power of Attorney.</u> First and foremost, this person should be someone who cares about you deeply. I often joke that I have named my sister-in-law to handle my finances because I think she would do very well at managing those. However, I am not sure she likes me enough that I would feel comfortable with her making my medical decisions. The person you choose to make your medical decisions does not need to have vast medical knowledge, but he or she does need to be a good listener. It will be important for them to listen to information from you as well as information from the various medical professionals they will encounter. They need to know your wishes concerning different medical situations. If you have religious preferences that are important to you, they should know and respect those. They also need to be a solid advocate for you, someone who is willing to stand up and fight for you if a provider is not taking appropriate care of you. There have been two instances in my life where this last point became increasingly apparent.

The first is with my wife's grandmother, Margie. Margie was a patient at a local hospital. Margie had suffered from a really bad infection and was battling delirium. Through the day, Margie had family with her constantly, and they had to keep reminding her that she couldn't get out of bed on her own as she was a fall risk. The hospital had a policy that ALL visitors had to leave at 8 pm and could not return until 8 am. My wife, Olivia, who happened to be Margie's Medical Power of Attorney, told the nurse that she was going to stay overnight. The nurse protested and brought in upper-management. Eventually, they relented allowing her to stay. Olivia placed her chair next to Margie's bed and physically stopped Margie from getting out of bed multiple times through the night. The nursing station was not close by, and the nurses would not have been in a position to keep a major fall from happening. Had Olivia not been a strong advocate, Margie would not have fared so well during that hospital stay. You need a strong advocate!

The next experience was during the birth of our twin boys. My wife complained through the night about the pain she was experiencing and stated she was in labor. The doctor on duty that night initially refused to come examine my wife, because the contractions were not being picked up by the machine. The nurse failed to advocate strongly for my wife and didn't believe her when she screamed that the pain was intense and she was clearly having contractions. Standing at my wife's bedside, I was dumbfounded by what was going on. Finally, at shift change, a new team came on board. I relayed all that had happened. The new doctor and new nurses took my wife in immediately for an emergency cesarean section. It still haunts me that I let it go as long as I did before I stood up and advocated for my wife. However, that experience taught me to never make that mistake again.

Be sure that your chosen advocate on your Medical Power of Attorney knows what you want and will advocate strongly for that level of care.

TRUTH 4

NO ONE WILL CARE FOR
YOUR KIDS THE WAY YOU DO,
BUT YOU CAN STILL MAKE
THE BEST AVAILABLE CHOICE

W](#)**ho should take the kids?** This question tends to be the one many of my clients wrestle with and the biggest reason people put off drafting a Will. Husbands and wives may not agree on the best choice or they may agree, but just can't bring themselves to share their decision with other family members for fear of hurt feelings. It may also be that you aren't sure who will be the best choice, but not making a decision only compounds the problem. If you have no plan in place, you may have competing family members battling it out in court. Court battles over custody of children often linger on for several years with no clear winners. Families are often forever torn in two as members feel forced to choose a side. Additionally, those legal battles can be extremely costly. Your estate should be left to care for your children - not pay lawyers to argue in court. Your children should be in a loving place where they can grieve - not in an emotional seesaw battle.

> **Accept the fact that there is not a perfect person. No one is going to do the job exactly as you would.**

Here are a few things to keep in mind as you make the decision. First, accept the fact that there is not a perfect person. No one is going to do the job exactly as you would. Second, you can name a different person to handle the money. If your sister is great with the kids but you don't trust her husband to be fair with money, then you can name someone else or a financial institution to manage the finances. Third, consider the needs of your child above all else. If Grandma is not the most capable person to take care of those needs, it is your responsibility to designate who is. It is important for you to decide exactly what is most important and choose the person you think will best continue those. Factors that should be considered when choosing this person are your values, whether that includes education, hard work, religious preferences, proximity to other family members, etc. I highly recommend that you communicate your wishes ahead of time. It is much better if family members know your wishes so there are no surprises. I had one client who had me prepare their estate plan several years ago, naming one of their best friends to serve in that role. They now wanted to change that as their friends had moved away. While they were still close, they no longer felt that their children would be best served by leaving their local community. They asked me to change their documents, but they didn't want to tell their friends that they were no longer the chosen guardians. I let them know it would be much better coming from them now, rather than their friends showing up in a tragedy to take care of the children and being turned away by the newly chosen guardians. Total transparency is a much better policy; even when it is hard.

TRUTH 5

ADULTS NEED WILLS

A Will does more than pass assets. A will plays a large part in letting your wishes be known when you can't be there to share your desires. Even if you don't have many assets, a Will can save your family frustration, time, money, and heartache. The Last Will and Testament allows you to control how your estate or probate assets will be distributed after you pass away. It also appoints the person who will administer your estate, and it may name a guardian for any minor children you have.

Probate assets can include your home, vehicles, cash, bank accounts, business interests, and all of your personal property.[3] The Last Will and Testament also enables you to create Trusts[4] for your beneficiaries as well as provide instructions on how to care for and distribute your property.

If you die without a valid Will, your property may be distributed by a court-appointed administrator according to a predetermined formula (defined by the State of Texas).

If you die without a valid Will, your property may be distributed by a court-appointed administrator according to a predetermined formula (defined by the State of Texas). Without a Will, you can't give your probate assets to a non-relative or even exclude certain relatives. If you do not have a Will and

---

3 See Truth #6 section below
4 See Truth #7 section below

there are no relatives at the time of your death, your property may go to the state.

The cost of probating a Will doesn't change much based on the size of the estate. You may not feel you have enough property to need a Will, but it is recommended for anyone over the age of eighteen. We do not know the time or circumstances that death will occur. I once sat with a family who lost their nineteen-year-old daughter in an automobile accident. The young lady did not have a Will or any estate planning documents. Her parents struggled with her apartment complex as they initially denied them entry to obtain belongings after her death as they did not have legal authority. Later, they faced a struggle obtaining their daughter's personal property from her crashed automobile. These are obstacles that should not exist when a family is grieving the loss of their loved one. Make it easier on your family by having a plan in place.

Often, it is more important for those with fewer assets to have a Will. It is a lot easier for a wealthy person to recover from a costly probate than someone who was counting on the assets for survival. Wills can be written in a variety of different ways to ensure that you are protected. I am often approached by clients telling me that their situation is uncomplicated and they just need a simple Will. This is usually before I hear that they are on their third marriage, have three children, are estranged from two of them, have a grandchild with a disability and they want to set up a Trust for their pets. We are all unique individuals, and your Will should be specifically tailored to your situation and your desires.

6

TRUTH

PROBATE STINKS

Most people assume that Probate is reserved for the estates of those individuals who never created a Will. While it's true that many cases of probate originate this way, it is not always the case. What is the probate process? Probate simply refers to the court managed process of settling an estate and distributing those assets to the intended beneficiaries. An Executor named in a Will has no authority until the Will has been offered to probate. Before we go through the probate process, let us explore the different types of assets. Probate assets are typically described as tangible things you can touch, feel and move around. Think of real estate, vehicles, personal property, businesses and that cash you have hidden in the mattress or buried in the backyard. Probate assets are controlled by your will. On the other hand, we have Non-probate assets. Think of bank accounts, life insurance, individual retirement accounts, annuities and brokerage accounts. Each of these accounts can have a named beneficiary. In the event of your death, the contract with the financial institution will determine who receive the money in the account. For example, if you hold an account as a joint tenancy with right of survivorship (JTWROS), the joint owner on the account will receive the funds in the account. If you have a payable on death (POD) or transfer on death (TOD) beneficiary named, the named beneficiary will receive the funds in that account. This happens regardless of what your will says, because the accounts are non-probate assets. However, if the account is held by only one person and there are no beneficiaries named, the account will be treated as a probate asset.

Peace Through Planning

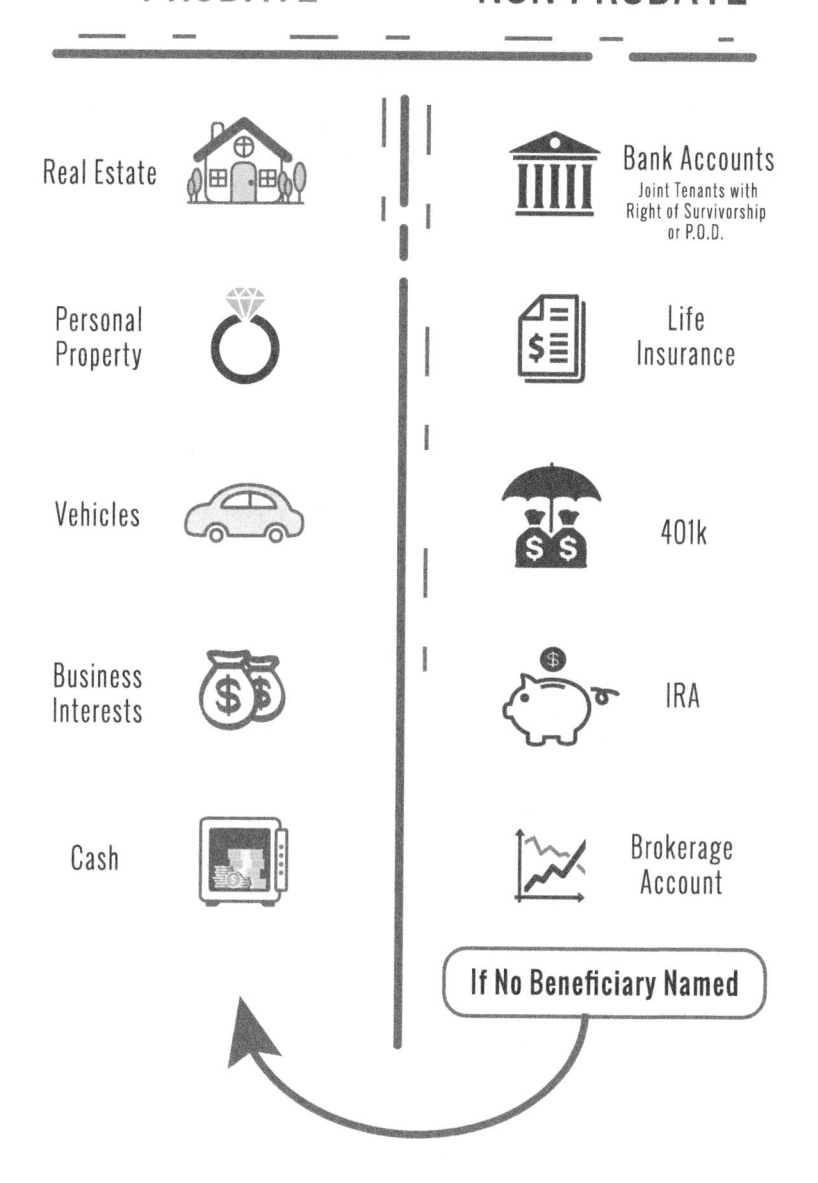

PROBATE | NON PROBATE

Probate:
- Real Estate
- Personal Property
- Vehicles
- Business Interests
- Cash

Non Probate:
- Bank Accounts — Joint Tenants with Right of Survivorship or P.O.D.
- Life Insurance
- 401k
- IRA
- Brokerage Account

If No Beneficiary Named → (goes to Probate)

Let's explore a case study based on the following example.

Bob and Sally have been married for 25 years. They have two children: Susan, who just turned 21, and John who just turned 14. Unfortunately, Bob recently passed away unexpectedly. Together, Bob and Sally owned a house which they purchased a few years ago, a couple of cars and they have joint bank accounts, retirement accounts, life insurance, and the stuff in their house. Bob and Sally also each have a bank account in their own name that they used for their "goofing off" money. Bob never got around to naming Sally as a beneficiary on his "goofing off" account. Bob and Sally completed Wills a few years back, so Sally knows there is a plan she needs to follow to take control of their assets. Sally is named as Executor and the only beneficiary of Bob's Will.

What is Sally's first step? She should gather as much information about their assets as possible and then meet with a Probate Attorney in her area. Together, they will put the assets into the two categories of Probate Assets and Non-Probate Assets.

Peace Through Planning

PROBATE

House   Cars

Stuff in House

(Bob's separate "Goofing Off" bank account with no benefiary)

NON PROBATE

Joint Bank Accounts

Retirement Accounts

Life Insurance

Now that we have split everything into these two categories, the attorney will likely tell Sally that she can contact the Life Insurance company, the retirement investment managers and the Bank holding the Joint Bank Accounts immediately. Once they receive a copy of Bob's death certificate, she will have no problem accessing those funds. The attorney will then help Sally start the Probate Process on the "probate assets".

Sally will need to have Bob's name removed from the house, cars, and the separate bank account so that she can decide to sell in the future, take a home equity loan or otherwise deal with the assets. So, the attorney will help Sally file an Application to Probate the Will. The court will post a notice that a Will has been offered to probate. (This notice gives others notification that if there is a later Will, or if they don't believe the Will is valid, they can contest it before it is admitted to probate.) After the notice has been posted for ten days, the court can hold a hearing where the Will is admitted to probate, the Executor is appointed officially by the court and the Executor takes an oath swearing to complete the tasks of an Executor. Since Sally is named in the Will as Executor, she will very likely be appointed by the court, assuming she doesn't have anything disqualifying her, such as a criminal background. After the hearing, Sally can start dealing with the property. She would normally notify beneficiaries (however, as the only beneficiary, she has no one to notify). Next, with the help of her attorney, she will prepare an inventory of the estate. This is basically a list of the property above in the "probate assets" category, plus any other property she learns of through the process. Her attorney will also help her publish a notice to creditors. Once she is satisfied that there are no debts to satisfy, she can distribute the bank account to herself, deed Bob's interest in the home to herself, and have Bob's interest in the cars transferred to herself.

The Probate Process can usually be handled with a single court hearing and often can be finished in a couple of months. This, of course, assumes that the Will is validly executed, and no one contests its validity. Beware that every state has a different probate process. This book focuses on the process in Texas.

Do I need an attorney to Probate a Will? While the law does not require it, many courts will insist that an Executor to be represented by an attorney. This is because an Executor has a fiduciary responsibility to the beneficiaries. Courts want Executors to understand the responsibility given to them. They must treat all beneficiaries with care and handle the estate always keeping the beneficiaries' best interest in mind. Even if your local court does not require an Executor to be represented by an attorney, it is good practice to do so. An Executor can be held personally liable if they mishandle creditors or the assets going to the beneficiaries. Beyond that, dealing with probate matters can be daunting. The process detailed above is a relatively simple situation but can be fraught with problems if you don't know which items are going to be appropriate in the inventory. There are also important time lines and deadlines to be aware of.

Can I avoid probate or does everyone have to go through it? Yes, probate can be avoided if you plan ahead.

Probate Process

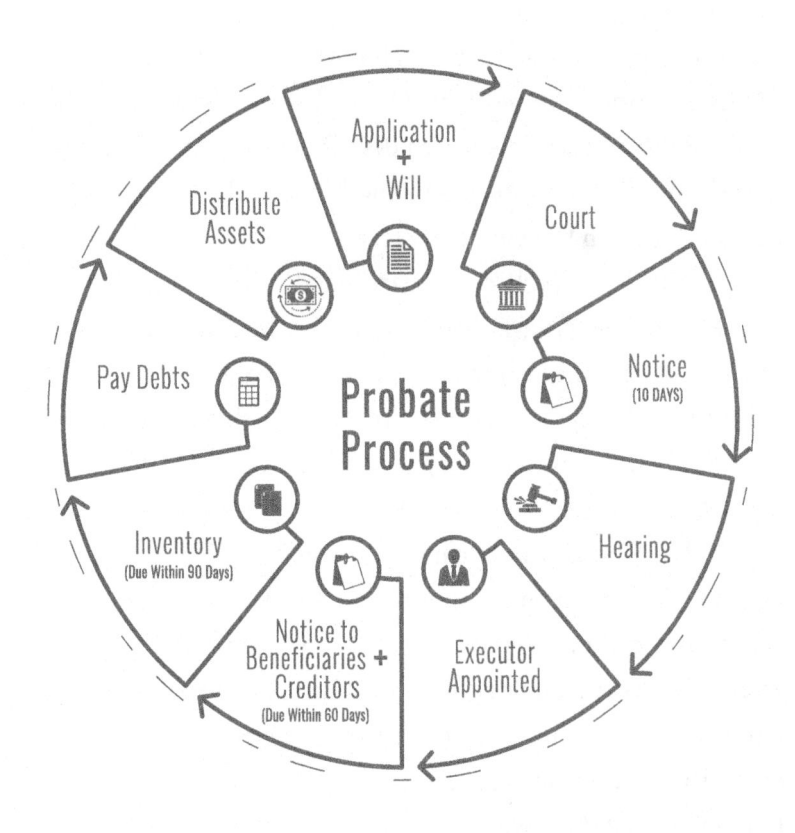

- Application + Will
- Court
- Notice (10 DAYS)
- Hearing
- Executor Appointed
- Notice to Beneficiaries + Creditors (Due Within 60 Days)
- Inventory (Due Within 90 Days)
- Pay Debts
- Distribute Assets

There are a multitude of avenues out there to avoid the probate process. They include the use of Revocable Living Trusts, Transfer of Death Deeds, Joint Bank Accounts, Deeds with Life Estates, etc. Once a person has passed away, it is often too late to avoid the probate process, but a probate attorney can help you navigate the process smoothly.

TRUTH 7

TRUSTS ARE
NEITHER SCARY
NOR EXPENSIVE

The word, "Trust" often leads people to think about extremely wealthy people and spoiled "Trust fund babies." However, Trusts are one of the most important tools in the Estate Planner's toolbox. At its most basic level, a Trust is simply a relationship between a Trustee and a beneficiary. The Trustee has the job of managing assets for the benefit of the beneficiary or beneficiaries. Trusts can be set up for many different reasons, including protecting an inheritance for a minor, tax avoidance, asset preservation, and probate avoidance. There is no one-size-fits-all Trust document. Each person or family has unique needs and desires. The Trust document should be carefully crafted to ensure those are met.

A Living Revocable Trust is a great tool to simplify your estate plan while you are living, and then peacefully transfer your estate to your beneficiaries after you pass away. The transfer of the estate is easier because the Revocable Trust eliminates the need to go through Probate of the decedent's estate. Probate is the legal process used to ensure the estate is handled properly after a person passes away. It involves making court appearances, paying debts, inventorying the estate, and dealing with creditors. The amount of time and money spent for Probate varies depending on the specific case; however, it is not uncommon for contested Probate cases to take several months, even years, and cost several thousand dollars. Many people who choose to create a Living Revocable Trust do so specifically to avoid Probate for their family members. They recognize the time and money they can save their family members in the future by setting up a Living Revocable Trust now. Consider whether or not you want your family dealing with the Probate process.

The Living Revocable Trust is created by the Grantor (the person who places property in the Trust) and the Trustee (the person who manages the property in the Trust) for the benefit of the beneficiary, (the party who benefits from the Trust). As the name of the Trust implies, it is fully revocable during the lifetime of the Grantor. This means the Grantor can make changes at any time. After the Trust is initially created, ownership of all of the Grantor's real and personal property are transferred into the name of the Trust. Houses, other real estate, bank accounts, and investment accounts can all be moved into the Trust.

Let us revisit Bob and Sally. Assume that instead of having a Will as the centerpiece of their plan, they instead drafted a Living Revocable Trust. They named each other as Co-Trustees and funded the Trust with their assets. They re-titled their

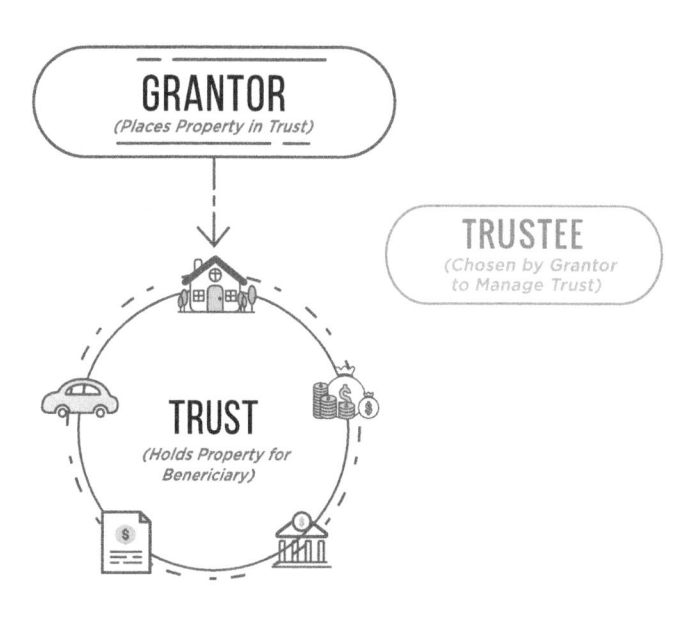

GRANTOR
(Places Property in Trust)

TRUSTEE
(Chosen by Grantor to Manage Trust)

TRUST
(Holds Property for Beneficiary)

home into the Trust, assigned their personal property and cars to the Trust and retitled their bank accounts to the Trust. Revisit the graphic to see where their assets are now.

As you can see, there are no longer any probate assets and therefore we are able to avoid probate court at Bob's death. When Bob passed away, Sally became the sole Trustee and sole beneficiary without ever having to present documents to a court. Through planning, Bob and Sally were able to simplify the work needed after Bob's death. Additionally, their children will be able to avoid going through probate at Sally's death as well.

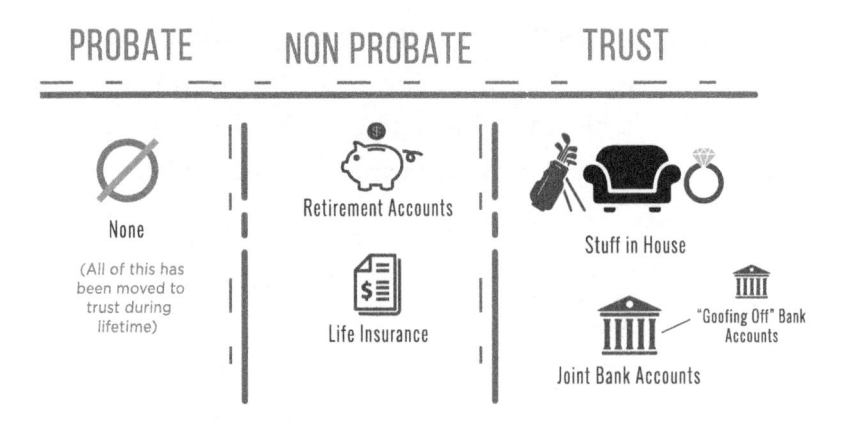

PROBATE

None

(All of this has been moved to trust during lifetime)

NON PROBATE

Retirement Accounts

Life Insurance

TRUST

Stuff in House

Joint Bank Accounts

"Goofing Off" Bank Accounts

Non-retirement accounts, like checking accounts, savings accounts and brokerage accounts can have the ownership changed to the Trust. However, retirement accounts, such as 401Ks and IRAs cannot be owned by a trust. They can have the Trust named as the pay-on-death beneficiary, so that the assets can be distributed according to the Trust. In most cases, life insurance policies are treated the same way and you are able to name the Trust as the beneficiary. Whether or not the Trust

Peace Through Planning

should be the primary beneficiary or just a contingent beneficiary is something that should be discussed with your Estate Planning Attorney as well as your Financial Advisor and tax professional. All of these accounts and properties continue to operate in the same manner as before without any change in tax status.[5] Most banks will allow you to keep the same account number as you had before retitling the account into the Trust. As property is sold or purchased, the titles to the properties are transferred into

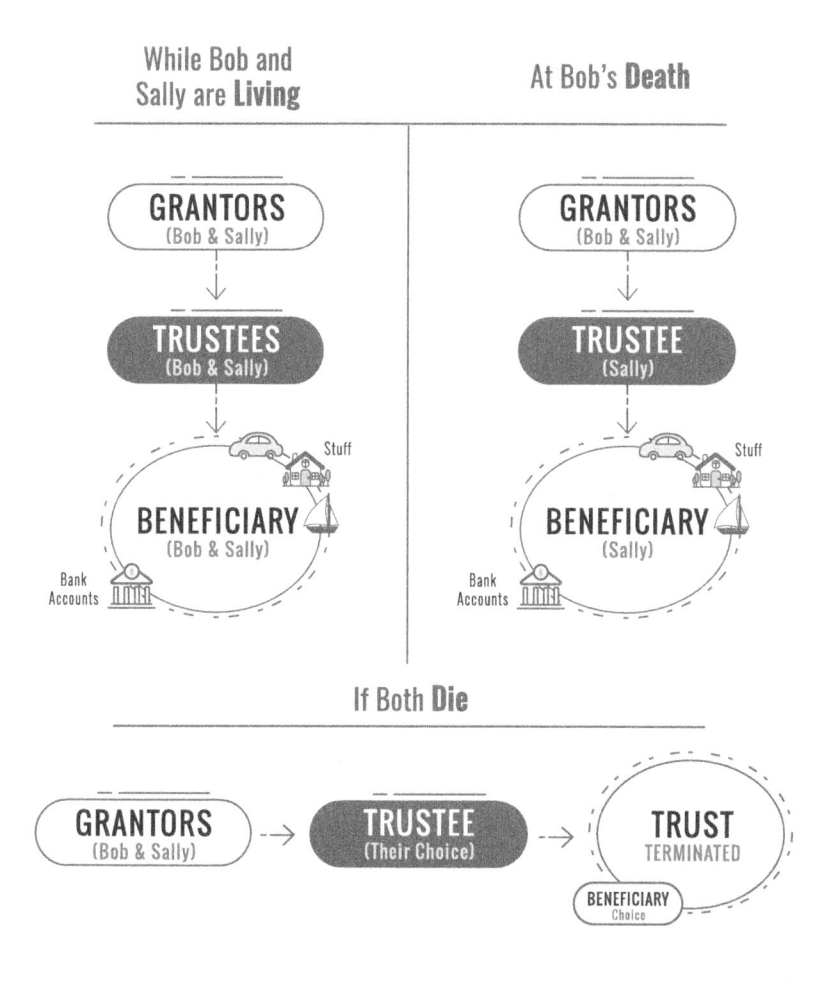

While Bob and Sally are Living

GRANTORS
(Bob & Sally)
↓
TRUSTEES
(Bob & Sally)
↓
BENEFICIARY
(Bob & Sally)

Bank Accounts, Stuff

At Bob's Death

GRANTORS
(Bob & Sally)
↓
TRUSTEE
(Sally)
↓
BENEFICIARY
(Sally)

Bank Accounts, Stuff

If Both Die

GRANTORS (Bob & Sally) → TRUSTEE (Their Choice) → TRUST TERMINATED
BENEFICIARY Choice

45

401k

The Trust Can be the BENEFICIARY

IRA

Insurance

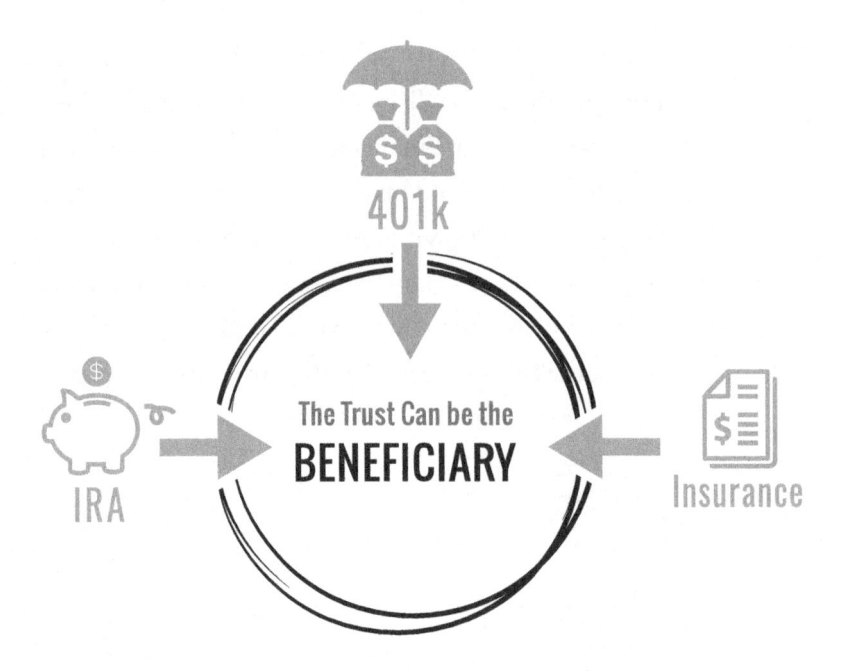

or out of the name of the Trust. When the Grantor passes away, the Trust can simply terminate so distributions can be made to the beneficiaries. There is no need to go through Probate because all the assets are still titled in the name of Trust.

Avoiding probate means that your business and financial situation remains private even after you are gone. People who own multiple pieces of real estate, real estate in more than one state, their own business, or even a share in a business should strongly consider a Living Revocable Trust. Additionally, people who simply want to protect their beneficiaries from having to deal with the probate process should consider a Living Revocable Trust.

---

[5] It is important for your Estate Planning Attorney to consult with your financial advisor to ensure that there are no unforeseen issues with taxation.

TRUTH 8

YOUR LAWYER
SHOULD KNOW
YOUR TEAM

When clients come to me, one of the first questions I ask them is who is on their team? Do they have a Certified Public Accountant (CPA), a financial advisor, a banker, business lawyer, etc? We don't live in a vacuum, so we don't practice estate planning that way either. The decisions that you make with your financial planner will affect your estate plan and the decisions you make with your estate plan may affect your taxes. We recommend that all of our clients work with a Certified Financial Planner. As Estate Planning attorneys, we can do a lot to protect your assets for those that you leave behind, but a financial advisor can help you make sure you are leaving enough behind to start with. As your estate increases in value, the help of a CPA is invaluable. They are there to make sure that you take advantage of all the tax benefits and don't get stuck paying more than you should to Uncle Sam. Your financial advisor, CPA, and attorney should all be working together to ensure that you are taken care of the best way possible. Your financial advisor should be discussing your beneficiary designations with your attorney to ensure that those beneficiary designations don't circumvent the purpose of the entire plan.

Take away one thing from this book: Get a plan in place that you understand!

CONCLUSION

The purpose of this book has been to demystify the world of Estate Planning, explain the importance of having a plan, and help give you some practical steps to get a plan in place. Take away one thing from this book: Get a plan in place that you understand! Having that plan in place will help you achieve peace knowing that you have done all you can to ensure that no matter what happens to you, your family will be able to continue living in their home, continue attending the same schools, and continue being loved by their family. They will survive, because you put the plan in place to ensure they do. Do not get hung up on details and let that keep you from making that initial appointment to get started. Pick an attorney you trust. Introduce them to the rest of your team. Name the folks in your life that you trust. Get the plan in place. Then, put it away and don't think about again until it is time for a review. This subject is not fun, but it is one of the most important subjects you will encounter. This is real life. Once you have the peace of knowing you have put the best plan together, you do not have to continue worrying about it. Review the plan yourself annually right after you do your taxes just to get it out of the way. If you see a red flag, call your Estate Planning Attorney to discuss. Otherwise, put it away and call your attorney for a review every five years. Congratulate yourself on achieving Peace Through Planning!

BONUS TRUTH 1

SPECIAL NEEDS
REQUIRE
SPECIAL PLANNING

If you have a child or family member with special needs, specific planning is necessary to ensure they are protected should something happen to you. Traditional gifting of money or property to a person with special needs can cause more harm than good. If you are thinking of leaving assets meant to benefit a person with special needs, items should be left in a Special or Supplemental Needs Trust to benefit the person as you intend.

The Supplemental Needs Trust is a very important part of every estate plan when there are potential beneficiaries who have a disability. Under current rules, a person can be disqualified from Medicaid and Social Security Benefits if they receive more than $2,000.00 in assets. In many cases, family members want to make a gift to the disabled person for their benefit. However, when not done properly, the gifts cause several problems. Creating a Supplemental Needs Trust to accept and manage the gifts ensure that the intended beneficiary will still receive the benefits of the gift without interrupting the Government programs that currently benefit them. The Supplemental Needs Trust is written so that those gifts may be used to Supplement rather than Supplant the Government Benefits.

The Irrevocable Living Supplemental Needs Trust is simply a Trust which a person creates while they are still living to benefit a child with special needs now and in the future. Let's explain it by breaking it down. First, irrevocable means that property and money gifted to the Trust cannot be recovered by the person making the gift. Anything put in the Trust becomes owned by the Trust and held for the benefit of the Beneficiary. Second, "Living" simply means that the Trust is created during the Grantor's lifetime and becomes its own entity. This means it will have a separate tax id number and file its own tax return should it earn any income. Third, "Supplemental Needs" simply means that it is set up for the benefit of a person with special needs with the proper provisions to ensure that the person is not disqualified from government benefits. Finally, "Trust" means that there is property held and used for the benefit of a beneficiary and managed by a Trustee. The Irrevocable Living Supplemental Needs Trust works great for people who foresee that others may also want to leave assets to the person whom they intend to benefit. You can set this Trust up now and let family and friends know where to make the gifts without disqualifying the person from government benefits.

A Testamentary Supplemental Needs Trust is included in a Last Will and Testament. The Last Will and Testament will state that the person with special needs shall not receive any property outright, but all property should be held and administered according to the Supplemental Needs Trust. The Testamentary Supplemental Needs Trust does not become active until the Last Will and Testament has been admitted to Probate. At that time, the Executor will establish the Trust, obtain the tax identification number for the Trust, and deposit property into the Trust. The named Trustee will then take over management of the trust property.

BONUS TRUTH 2

THE ESTATE TAX WILL NOT DIRECTLY AFFECT MOST AMERICANS

What about the estate/death/inheritance tax? The Estate Tax is known by many different names, and strikes fear into the hearts of many investors and beneficiaries. Everyone wants to know how much of their money Uncle Sam is going to take. The Tax Reform Act of 2018 has reduced that stress and worry substantially. As of January 1, 2019, an individual can now pass up to 11.4 million dollars worth of assets during their lifetime or at their death (no double dipping) with no estate tax liability. Let me repeat that, ZERO tax liability on transfers up to 11.4 million dollars for an individual. A married couple can double that amount. This means that less than one-half of one percent of Americans who die will pay any estate tax. This number will be adjusted annually to keep up with inflation. It is also important to note that this part of the Tax Reform Act of 2018 expires in the year 2025. At that time, the exemption will be cut back in half to reflect the law on the books before the act was passed. Therefore, folks with Estates above roughly 5 million dollars should still consider methods of reducing their estate tax liability.

> **As of January 1, 2019, an individual can now pass up to 11.4 million dollars worth of assets during their lifetime or at their death (no double dipping) with no estate tax liability.**

PRE-PLANNING WORKSHEET

This document can help you begin to take some notes as you get ready for your initial meeting with an Estate Planning Attorney. This document is not intended to be a substitute for legal counsel and cannot serve as a substitute for a Will or Trust.

ESTATE PLANNING QUESTIONNAIRE

HELPING YOU ACHIEVE
PEACE THROUGH PLANNING

> Drafting an Estate Plan is one of the most important and loving gifts that you give to those who are important to you. Every person who has attained age 18 needs to have a Will, a Durable Power of Attorney, a Medical Power of Attorney, a HIPAA Release, and a Directive to Physicians (aka living will). People often believe that "ESTATE PLANNING" is only for the wealthy. This is not true. In fact, it is often more important for persons who are not so wealthy to plan as not having a plan can be very expensive for you and your loved ones.
>
> When you first look at this document you might feel overwhelmed, don't worry if you can't finish, we will help you when you come in for your consultation.

Estate - Everything that you own including land, cars, possessions, digital assets, and other assets.

Will - A document which provides who is to receive your property, who will administer your estate, who will serve as guardian of your children, if applicable, and other provisions.

1. Full Name

___

Name

___

All other names by which you have been known

___ ☐ Male ☐ Female
Age   Date of Birth (DOB)

___

Are you a U.S. citizen?

___

If no, country of Citizenship

2. Current Residence

___

Street Address

___

City

___

State   County   Zip

___

Phone   Alt Phone

___

Email

3. If you are married, your spouse's full name

_____
Full Name

_____
All other names by which you have been known

_____   ☐ Male ☐ Female
Age   Date of Birth(DOB)

_____
Date of Marriage

_____
Place of Marriage

_____
Are you currently living with your spouse?

_____
Phone   Alt Phone

_____
Email

4. Do you and your spouse have a Pre-Nuptial Agreement which identifies and disposes of separate spousal property?

Full Name

All other names by which you have been known

Age   Date of Birth (DOB)   ☐ Male ☐ Female

Are you a U.S. citizen?

If no, country of Citizenship

5. If either of you or your spouse have been divorced, please answer the following:

If yes, which spouse?

Date of Marriage   Date of Divorce   Date of Spouse's Death (if applicable)

6. Have you or your spouse created any trusts or made gifts though trusts to other?

If yes, describe and include a copy

7. Do you or your spouse expect any inheritance? If yes, state from whom and amount expected.

_____

8. Do you or your spouse expect any inheritance? If yes, state from whom and how much.

_____

1. Full Name

Son/Daughter	DOB	Child of Current Marriage

_____

If no, Name of Other Parent

_____

2. Full Name

Son/Daughter	DOB	Child of Current Marriage

_____

If no, Name of Other Parent

_____

3. Full Name

Son/Daughter	DOB	Child of Current Marriage

_____

If no, Name of Other Parent

4. Full Name

Son/Daughter DOB Child of Current Marriage

If no, Name of Other Parent

5. Full Name

Son/Daughter DOB Child of Current Marriage

If no, Name of Other Parent

Intellectual disability - a disability characterized by significant limitations both in intellectual functioning and in adaptive behavior which covers many everyday social and practical skills.

9. Are any of your children or other beneficiaries intellectually or physically disabled or have special needs?

If so, note any special provisions

If so, are they presently receiving, or do you anticipate that they may apply for, SSI benefits in the future?

Note: If you leave a bequest, directly to a beneficiary the recipient might be disqualified from SSI benefits.

10.(a) Deceased Biological or legally adopted children if applicable

_____

1. Full Name

_____   _____   _____
Son/Daughter   DOB   Child of Current Marriage

_____

2. Full Name

_____   _____   _____
Son/Daughter   DOB   Child of Current Marriage

10.(b) Deceased child's living children if applicable

_____

1. Full Name

_____   _____   _____
Son/Daughter   DOB   Child of Current Marriage

_____

2. Full Name (First, Middle, Last)

_____   _____   _____
Son/Daughter   DOB   Child of Current Marriage

11. If you have grandchildren, state the following for each. If not, continue to question 12.

1. Full Name

Grandson/Granddaughter   DOB
                                    Living

2. Full Name

Grandson/Granddaughter   DOB
                                    Living

3. Full Name

Grandson/Granddaughter   DOB
                                    Living

12. (a) If your children are under the age of 18, state the following for the person you wish to act as their guardian in the event of your death or in case of the joint death of you and your spouse.

Name

Relationship

Address

12. (b) If at the time of your death the person named above is unwilling to serve as guardian, please list an alternative:

_____
Name

_____
Relationship

_____
Address

13. Indicate how you want your assets to pass at your death. *Please check the ONE option you prefer:*

Option A:
I want my assets to pass to my spouse and children as follows:

To my spouse, if surviving.

If my spouse predeceases me, my assets will be divided in equal shares to my children.

If any of my children predecease me, that child's share shall be distributed to his or her children in equal shares.

_____

_____

Option B:
I am unmarried with children and want my assets to pass as follows:

In equal shares to my children

If one or more of my children predeceases me, that child's share in my estate is distributed to his or her children in equal shares.

In the event all my children and descendants fail to survive me, I want my assets to be distributed as follows:

_____

_____

Option C:
None of the above. I want my assets to pass as follows:

_____

_____

_____

****If you leave real property with a mortgage the property will pass to the beneficiary named in your Will, subject to the mortgage. If you want to be free and clear of debt, you must direct that other assets pay off the debt, provided there are sufficient assets available****

Executor - A person who is appointed by a testator to execute the testator's wishes laid out in a Will.

14. Who do you want named as Executor of the estate?

_____

Full Name

_____

(First Alternative) Full name

_____

(Second Alternative) Full name

15. If you are married, your spouse's Executor

_____

Full Name

_____

(First Alternative) Full name

_____

(Second Alternative) Full name

Trustee - A person who controls property or money for the benefit of another person.

16. Who do you want to be the Trustee of any trusts, if applicable?

_____

Full Name

_____

(First Alternative) Full name

_____

(Second Alternative) Full name

17. If you are married, your spouse's trustee:

_____

Full Name

_____

(First Alternative) Full name

_____

(Second Alternative) Full name

Durable Power of Attorney - This document gives the person or persons named, the power to handle your financial affairs. The person(s) you choose must be someone you trust to make all your financial decisions. Its power is extinguished upon your death.

18. Who do you want to name as agent on your Durable Power of Attorney?

Full Name

Address

Phone Number   Relationship

(First Alternative) Full name

Address

Phone Number   Relationship

(Second Alternative) Full name

Address

Phone Number   Relationship

19. If you are married, your Spouse's agents

Full Name

Address

Phone Number   Relationship

(First Alternative) Full name

Address

Phone Number   Relationship

(Second Alternative) Full name

Address

Phone Number   Relationship

Medical Power of Attorney - This document gives the person or persons named the power to make medical decisions in the event you are not able to. They will be able to confer with medical personnel and make decisions on your behalf.

20. Who would you like to name as agent on your Medical Power of Attorney?

Full Name

Address

Phone Number   Relationship

(First Alternative)

Address

Phone Number   Relationship

(Second Alternative)

Address

Phone Number   Relationship

21. If you are married, your Spouse's agents

Full Name

Address

Phone Number   Relationship

(First Alternative)

Address

Phone Number   Relationship

(Second Alternative)

Address

Phone Number   Relationship

HIPAA Release - This document releases health information to those you designate.

22. Did you want to include any other persons on the separate HIPAA release?

_____

Full Name

_____

Address

_____   _____

Phone Number   Relationship

23. If you are married, does your spouse wish to include any other persons on the separate HIPAA release?

_____

Full Name

_____

Address

_____   _____

Phone Number   Relationship

24. Do you want an Advanced Directive (commonly called a living will)?

☐ Yes   ☐ No

---

25. Do you want to complete an Organ Donation Form?

☐ Yes   ☐ No

---

26. Do you plan to be buried or cremated? Do you want to be buried in a specific location? Or in the case of cremation do you want your ashes spread in a specific location?

To learn more or to download questionnaire visit:
www.peacethroughplanning.com

Description of Asset:	Individual Assets (Dollar Amounts)	Spouses's Separate Assets	Community Assets (Dollar Amounts)	Beneficiaries
Home				
Other Real Estate				
Bank Accounts				
1.				
2.				
3.				
4.				
Automobiles				
1.				
2.				
3.				
401k Plans or Qualified Retirement Plan				
1.				
2.				
3.				
Stocks, Mutual Funds & Other Investments				
1.				
2.				
3.				
Business Interests				
Life Insurance				
Miscellaneous Collectibles				
Totals				

PEACE THROUGH PLANNING

The wonderful feeling you have after having your estate plan prepared by a qualified attorney.

Charles Weisinger

Notes

Peace Through Planning

Charles Weisinger

GLOSSARY OF TERMS

The following is a list of terms regularly used when discussing Estate Planning and Probate. These terms are defined by me in simple terms. If you want the official definitions, please refer to a legal dictionary such as Black's Law Dictionary.

Administrator:
A person appointed by a court to close up the business of an estate and ensure that the proper heirs receive the property of a decedent. Administrators are much like Executors and usually used in situations where there is no Will or the named Executor in a Will cannot serve.

Agent:
A person named in a power of attorney document tasked with carrying out the actions outlined in the document.

Beneficiary:
The person who is to receive property under a Will, a Trust, or life insurance.

Chaos:
The absence of Peace. This is the feeling you leave behind if you don't have a plan in place.

Decedent:
The person who died.

Durable Power of Attorney:
This document gives the person or persons named, the power to handle your financial affairs. The person(s) you choose must be someone you trust to make all your financial decisions. Its power is extinguished upon your death.

Estate:
Everything that you own including land, cars, possessions, and digital assets.

Estate Plan:
A plan that dictates what should happen to you and your assets in the case of incapacity or death. The plan also lays out who should take care of your children in the case you are no longer able.

Executor:
The person named and tasked with the duty of carrying out the terms of a Will.

Guardian:
A person who has been appointed by the court to care for and manage the estate or person of another. The Guardian will have annual reporting requirements with the court.

Guardianship:
The process by which a court removes the rights of one person so that another may handle their decisions for them. This is usually due to issues of incapacity. Additionally, Guardians can be appointed for minors. A parent is the natural Guardian of the person for a minor, however, a parent must apply to the court if there is an Estate to manage.

Grantor:
The person who grants property to a Trust. Synonyms: Trustor, Settlor, Trustmaker

Heirs:
In the absence of a Will, the people who are entitled to receive a decedent's estate.

HIPAA:
The Health Insurance Portability and Accountability Act. This is the act that makes all of our health information private. A HIPAA release is needed so that your loved ones can access your medical information.

Intestate:
Dying without a Will.

Irrevocable:
This typically refers to a Trust that cannot be changed or amended. Once the document is signed, it is no longer able to be changed, except in certain limited circumstances.

Letters of Administration:
The document that a court gives to an Administrator after an order creating an Administration has been signed. These letters allow the Administrator to carry out the business of distributing assets and wrapping up an estate.

Letters Testamentary:
The document that a court gives to an Executor after a will has been admitted to probate. These letters allow the Executor to

carry out the business of distributing assets and wrapping up an estate.

Medical Power of Attorney:
This document gives the person or persons named the power to make medical decisions in the event you are not able to. They will be able to confer with medical personnel and make decisions on your behalf.

Peace Through Planning:
The feeling you get knowing that you have done everything you can to take care of your family in the case of a tragedy.

Power of Attorney:
A legal document by which a Principal gives another person (called an agent) the ability to handle certain things on their behalf. Powers of Attorney can be drafted for making medical or financial decisions.

Probate:
The legal process by which a court determines where a decedent's assets should go after their death.

Revocable:
A document that can be modified, changed, deleted at anytime by the parties that created it.

Settlor:
See Grantor

Testate:
Dying with a Will.

Testator:
A person making a Will.

Trust:
An agreement between a Grantor and a Trustee for the benefit of a Beneficiary. A Grantor gives property to a Trustee who manages it for the benefit of the Beneficiary.

Trustee:
The person tasked with managing assets in a Trust for the benefit of the Beneficiary.

Trustor:
See Grantor

Will:
A document that directs where your probate assets go after you pass away.

ABOUT THE AUTHOR

Charles Weisinger is the Founder and Managing Attorney of Weisinger Law Firm PLLC. Charles is Board Certified in Estate Planning and Probate Law by the Texas Board of Legal Specialization and is an Accredited Estate Planner with National Association of Estate Planners and Councils. He has been named a Texas Rising Star for 2018 and 2019 by Texas Super Lawyers.

Charles is passionate about helping families avoid the confusion and chaos that can come when someone dies without an Estate Plan in place. He manages a firm of attorneys who have made it their mission to serve families with Integrity, Consistency and Excellence while helping them achieve Peace Through Planning®.

Charles lives in San Antonio, Texas with his wife, Olivia, and their four children.

> To learn more or to download questionnaire visit:
> www.peacethroughplanning.com

HERE IS WHAT PROFESSIONALS ARE SAYING ABOUT PEACE THROUGH PLANNING

Peace Through Planning tackles an extremely important topic and gives a plan to achieve peace of mind. With a blended family and an adult child with special needs, we know the importance of having a plan specific to us. Charlie was instrumental in guiding us through the process of setting up our estate plan. I sleep better at night knowing my family is protected and we can fulfill our wishes for our children.

Kameron Chicoine
Managing Editor of Exceptional Kids Magazine: A Resource Guide for the Special Needs Community and Managing Editor of Senior Living Choices

Charlie Weisinger has addressed the basics we all need to know, but too often are reluctant to ask about. I'm regularly surprised at how many business owners I work with who have ignored the need for an orderly transition of their companies and their personal assets. Peace Through Planning is written for those who are "too busy" to address their families' security. It's logical, plain-spoken and clearly communicates how much Charlie cares about helping people.

John F. Dini
Author of Your Exit Map: Navigating the Boomer Bust

Weisinger makes it so much easier to digest and understand the intimidating topic of estate planning. This book is perfect for those of us who don't want to be a burden on friends and family.

Darryl W. Lyons
Co-founder of PAX Financial Group, LLC and author of 18 to 80: A Simple and Practical Guide to Money and Retirement for all Ages

POWER HOUSE
PUBLISHING

ALEXANDRIA
VIRGINIA

Made in the USA
Middletown, DE
23 March 2025